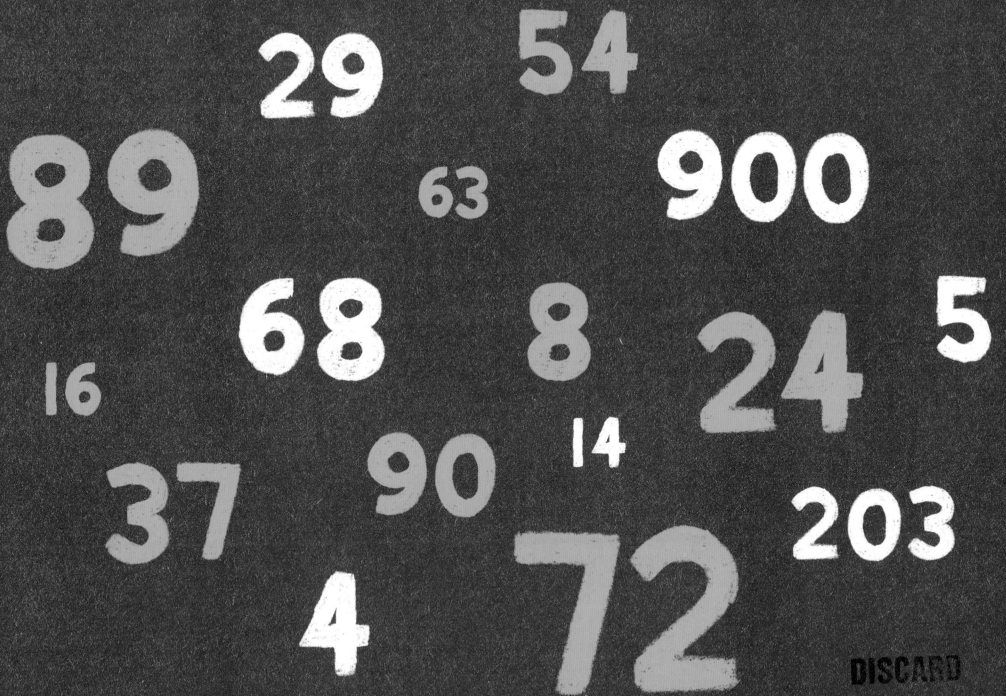

For Adam and Wyatt —L. M. S.

Special thanks for their generous consultation in the making of this book to:
Daniel F. Culbert, University of Florida Cooperative Extension, Okeechobee, Florida
Timothy Layser, Wildlife Biologist, Selkirk Conservation Alliance, Priest River, Idaho
Charlotte Goldston, High Meadow Alpacas, Franklin, Tennessee
Joe deGraauw, Avian Curator, Nashville Zoo at Grassmere, Nashville, Tennessee
Kevin Torregrosa, Reptile Curator, St. Augustine Alligator Farm, St. Augustine, Florida
Jessica Munson, Milwaukee County Zoo, Milwaukee, Wisconsin
Mary Stella, Dolphin Research Center, Grassy Key, Florida
Chris Hartley, Sophia M. Sachs Butterfly House, Missouri Botanical Garden, Chesterfield, Missouri
Steven L. Bailey, Curator of Fishes, New England Aquarium, Boston, Massachusetts
Diane F. Cowan, PhD, Founder, Executive Director & Senior Scientist, The Lobster
  Conservancy, Friendship, Maine
Randy Scheer, Animal Curator, Lincoln Children's Zoo, Lincoln, Nebraska

Library of Congress Cataloging-in-Publication Data:

Schaefer, Lola M., 1950-
Lifetime: the amazing numbers in animal lives / by Lola M. Schaefer ; illustrated by Christopher Silas Neal
pages cm.
Audience: Ages 4-8.
Audience: Grades K to grade 3.
ISBN 978-1-4521-0714-1 (alk. paper)
1. Developmental biology—Juvenile literature. 2. Life expectancy—Juvenile literature. 3. Animals—
Pictorial works—Juvenile literature. I. Neal, Christopher Silas, illustrator. II. Title.
QH491.S34 2013
591.56—dc23
2012039328

Design by Amelia May Mack.
Typeset in Pluto.
The illustrations in this book were rendered in mixed media.

Manufactured in China.

10 9 8 7 6 5 4 3 2

Chronicle Books LLC
680 Second Street, San Francisco, California 94107

Chronicle books—we see things differently. Become part of
our community at www.chroniclekids.com.

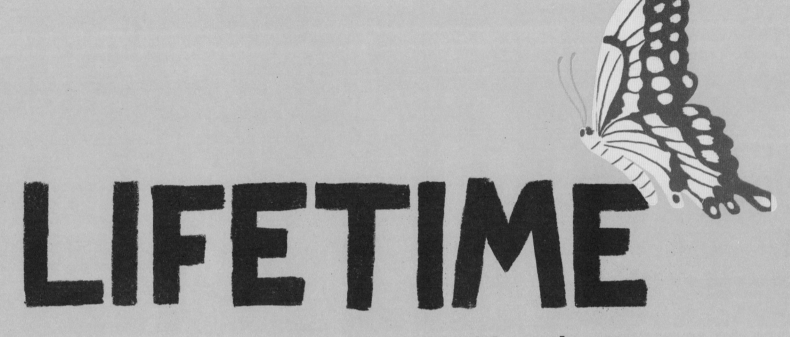

LIFETIME

The Amazing Numbers
in Animal Lives

by **Lola M. Schaefer** illustrated by **Christopher Silas Neal**

chronicle books·san francisco

95

202

4

64

39

2

567

72

14

130

83

60

28

45

9

Lifetime shows how many times one particular animal performs one behavior or grows one feature in a lifetime. I based the estimations on the average adult life span of each wild animal that lives to maturity and the recorded and observational information about its behaviors or physical appearance. Of course, just about every animal in one species will be a little different. Circumstances vary due to weather, habitat, enemies, pollution, hunting, and available food. But I spoke with experts at zoos, aquaria, conservation centers, and universities to compute the most accurate approximations possible. Enjoy reading and . . . counting! —Lola

In one lifetime,
    this spider will spin
1 papery egg sac.

Fragile. Don't touch!

In one lifetime,
this caribou will grow
and shed
10 sets of antlers.

In one lifetime,
   this alpaca will grow
20 different fleeces.

Never chilly in
this warm coat!

In one lifetime,
this woodpecker will
drill **30** roosting
holes in the woods.

Rat-a-tat-tat-tat-tat!

In one lifetime, this rattlesnake will add **40** beads to its rattle.

If you can hear this rattle, you are TOO close!

In one lifetime,
this female red kangaroo
will birth **50** joeys.

*So many
hoppy birthdays!*

In one lifetime,
  this bottlenose dolphin
will use the same **100** teeth
    to grab food from the sea.

The slipperier, the better!

In one lifetime,
this giraffe will grow
200 inches
(508 centimeters)
tall and . . .

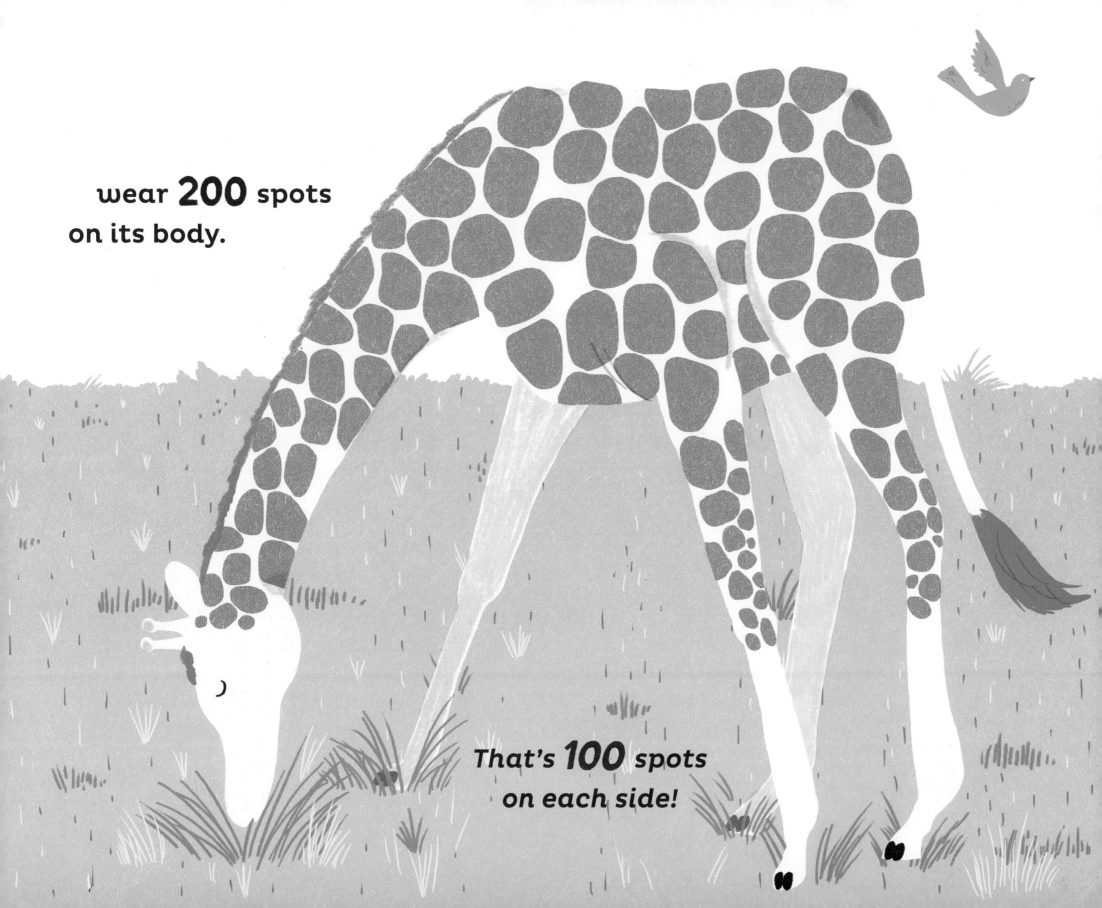

wear **200** spots on its body.

That's **100** spots on each side!

In one lifetime,
this alligator will
build **22** nests
and lay **550** eggs.

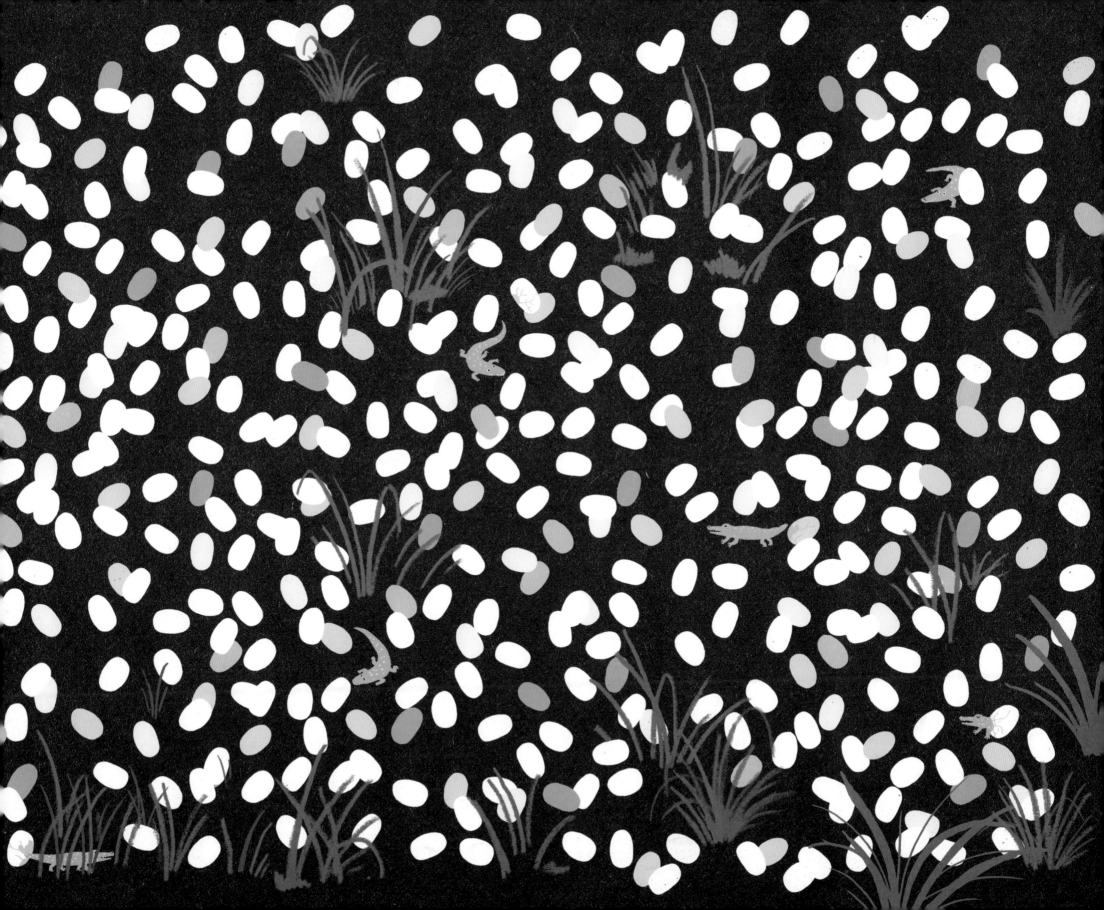

In one lifetime,
this giant swallowtail will visit
900 flowers, sipping nectar.

Sweet.

In one lifetime,
this male seahorse
will carry and birth
1,000 teeny-weeny,
squiggly-wiggly
baby seahorses.

17

58

6

99

46

75

29

120

90

4

77

63

52

33

80

291

THE ANIMALS

Cross Spider *Araneus diadematus*

The cross spider received its name because of a pattern of white dots on its back that forms a cross. It is a common garden spider that can be found in Europe and North America. The female will spin many large circular orb-webs in her lifetime. When an insect becomes trapped in her web, the spider wraps the prey in silk, injects it with venom, and eats it.

In early autumn, the female leaves the web and finds a protected spot, like a crack or small opening, to spin 1 egg sac full of tiny spider eggs. In a few days, the female spider will die, but come spring, between 300 and 900 spiderlings will hatch.

Average Adult Life Span: 6 months. Females produce 1 egg sac (cocoon) in a lifetime.

Our example: 1 cross spider lifetime × 1 egg sac = 1

Mountain Caribou *Rangifer tarandus*

Most mountain caribou live in British Columbia, Canada, but a few travel into the states of Washington, Idaho, and Montana and then back again into Canada. Both female and male mountain caribou grow antlers (though the females' antlers are much smaller). The males grow their first full sets near the age of 2. Mountain caribou will grow and shed 1 set of antlers each year.

Antlers begin as a bony growth, then become covered with a thin layer of skin and hair, called velvet. The antlers grow quickly and within 3 to 4 months the antlers have reached full size.

Male caribou grow antlers in the late spring/early summer. They use them in the fall when fighting other males during mating season, and then shed them in the winter. Female caribou grow their antlers in late fall/early winter and shed them in summer.

Average Adult Life Span: 8 to 12 years

Our example: 12 years in a caribou lifetime – 2 years before the caribou will grow antlers = 10 years in which the caribou will grow and shed antlers.

10 years in which the caribou will shed antlers × 1 set of antlers per year = 10 sets of antlers in a lifetime.

Alpaca *Vicugna pacos*

In the wild, alpacas graze on vegetation at altitudes of 11,500 to 16,000 feet (3,505 to 4,877 meters) across several South American countries. To protect themselves from the cold temperatures in those high places, these animals grow a coat, similar to sheep's wool, which is thick and soft.

In the wild, alpacas grow just 1 fleece and use it all of their lives. But when alpacas are raised on farms, people shear the alpacas once a year, when the weather warms in the spring. The fleece is then made into yarns or other strands to be woven into blankets, coats, hats, sweaters, and even gloves.

Average Adult Life Span: 20 to 21 years

Our example: 20 years in an alpaca lifetime × 1 fleece per year = 20 fleeces in a lifetime.

Pileated Woodpecker *Dryocopus pileatus*

Pileated woodpeckers are 1 of the largest common woodpeckers in North America. They drill 3 to 4 roosting holes and 1 nesting hole each year in old or dead trees. Roosting holes are much smaller than nesting holes—just big enough for 1 bird to roost comfortably. (Nesting holes have to be large enough for a nest, a woodpecker, and woodpecker chicks.) Roosting holes are used occasionally for short daytime naps, but are most important during the night for safety, resting, or sleeping. Pileated woodpeckers often drill a roosting hole close to their nesting holes so the male and female can take turns caring for the eggs.

Pileated woodpeckers also peck occasional holes in trees to find food. But unlike sapsucker woodpeckers, which riddle trees with holes, pileated woodpeckers prefer to eat insects off the surface of trees or strip sections of bark in search of ants.

Average Adult Life Span: 10 years

Our example: 10 years in a pileated woodpecker lifetime - 1 year to mature = 9 years.

If the woodpecker drills 3 to 4 roosting holes a year, the average is 3½ roosting holes per year. 9 years of roosting in a woodpecker lifetime × 30½ holes drilled per year = 31½ (which we've approximated as 30) holes drilled in a lifetime.

Eastern Diamondback Rattlesnake *Crotalus adamanteus*

The eastern diamondback rattlesnake is the largest venomous snake in North America. It lives in dry or sandy habitats from North Carolina down to Florida and west to Louisiana. Like other snakes, this snake sheds its skin as it grows in size. Each time it sheds, the scales on its tail form a new bead. The snake sheds its skin more often in the first 4 years of its life, because it grows more quickly when it is young.

The bead is a hard, hollow segment. When the eastern diamondback rattlesnake feels threatened, it shakes its beads—this is the rattle—as a warning to stay away. As this snake ages, its tail adds 10, 20, 30, or even 40 more beads. It would be unusual, though, to see an eastern diamondback rattlesnake with all 40 beads on its rattle because the older beads near the tip of the tail break off easily when rubbed against rocks or dry earth.

Average Adult Life Span: 18 to 25 years

Our example: Assuming our snake lives 24 years, it will have 20 shedding cycles in the first 4 years of life and 1 shedding cycle per year for the rest of its life.

24 years of life - 4 = 20—that is, 20 shedding cycles in the rest of its life.

20 shedding cycles in its first 4 years + 20 shedding cycles in the rest of its lifetime = 40 shedding cycles—and thus 40 beads added to its tail—in its lifetime.

Red Kangaroo *Macropus rufus*

Red kangaroos are marsupials and live in the wild in the scrublands and deserts of Australia. A female red kangaroo matures at about 18 months. She can then birth her first joey (a baby kangaroo), which weighs approximately the same as two raisins. This joey climbs into the female's pouch, where it will remain for 6 to 8 months. When it leaves, the female will continue to nurse that joey. Meanwhile, the female will give birth to another joey who will ride in her pouch. The female may even become pregnant with a third joey. So it's possible for a female to support 3 joeys at the same time. Most female red kangaroos will birth 2 to 3 joeys each year.

Average Adult Life Span: 21.5 years

Our example: 21½ years in a red kangaroo lifetime - 1½ years to mature = 20 years. If she has 2 to 3 joeys per year, let's average that to 2½ per year.

20 years of having joeys × 2½ joeys per year = 50 joeys in a lifetime.

Bottlenose Dolphin *Tursiops truncatus*

A bottlenose dolphin is a mammal that lives in the ocean. But unlike other mammals, this animal uses the same set of teeth for its entire life—it has no baby teeth. A bottlenose dolphin will grow 72 to 104 teeth and each tooth is shaped like a small cone. However, most of these dolphins have 100 teeth. Conical teeth grab and hold slippery fish better than any other shape. Since this dolphin swallows its food whole, there's no need for teeth that chop, tear, or grind. But these teeth do have another use. A dolphin is a social animal, and uses its teeth to scratch or "rake" the skin of other dolphins during play.

Average Adult Life Span: Varies greatly. Many dolphins can live to be 50 years old, however great numbers die in the first 10 years of their lives due to predators, disease, or pollution.

Our example: A dolphin that has 100 teeth—50 in the upper jaw and 50 in the lower.

Giraffe *Giraffa camelopardalis reticulata*

Giraffes are the tallest animals in the world. They live in parts of the central and southern savannahs of Africa. Their height helps them reach their favorite food—acacia leaves— high in the treetops. An adult giraffe's neck is about 6 feet (1.8 meters) long and each leg measures about 6 feet (1.8 meters) tall. Males can reach a height of 18 feet (5.5 meters). Females grow to be near 17 feet (5.2 meters) tall.

During a birth, the female giraffe stands and the young giraffe drops 6 feet (1.8 meters) to the ground, but doesn't get hurt. It quickly stands. The calf is already 6 feet (1.8 meters) tall!

The reticulated giraffe has a pattern of spots on its hide that looks like a lacy network. The word *reticulated* means *net* or *network*. This giraffe has brown box-shaped figures that form a pattern all over its skin. The white spaces in between the boxes look like white lines, or a net. Like our fingerprints, no 2 patterns are ever quite the same. Most adult reticulated giraffes have between 185 and 215 spots on their hide.

Average Adult Life Span: 15 to 22 years

Our example: A female giraffe that stands 200 inches/16⅔ feet (500 centimeters) tall and has 200 spots.

American Alligator *Alligator mississippiensis*

An American alligator lives in the freshwater swamps, lakes, and rivers of the southeast United States. This reptile is a great swimmer and can also run on land, even though it weighs 800 to 1,000 pounds (363 to 454 kilograms).

A female alligator usually lives to be 30 to 75 years old. After she matures (which takes about 6 years), she will begin to have babies. She will build a nest out of moist vegetation, sticks, mud, or reeds near the water. If all resources were available in the wild, and the female and male could find one another each year, the female could build 1 nest a year. But since that's not the case for most females, the average nesting behavior is that she will build 1 nest every other year.

She will lay 20 to 60 eggs in each nest and cover them with more dead plant life. The decaying vegetation makes heat that keeps the eggs warm. The female guards the nest for 2 months while the baby alligators grow in their eggs. After 2 months, the baby alligators, or hatchlings, emerge. The hatchlings are 6 to 8 inches (15 to 20 centimeters) long. A female American alligator could lay as few as 300 eggs and as many as 900 eggs in one lifetime.

Average Adult Life Span: 30 to 75 years

Our example: 50 years in an alligator lifetime - 6 years to begin having babies = 44 years in which the alligator could have babies. But she only laid eggs every 2 years, so 44 ÷ 2 = 22 years in which the alligator laid eggs.

Let's say she laid an average of 25 eggs each time. 22 times she laid eggs × 25 eggs each time = 550 eggs in a lifetime.

Giant Swallowtail *Papilio cresphontes*

The giant swallowtail butterfly lives year-round in countries in Central and South America, as well as in Florida. In other parts of North America, it is a seasonal visitor (in the summer months).

The female swallowtail lays eggs on plants such as prickly ash and orange trees. Just like other butterflies, the giant swallowtail visits flowers to sip nectar. It enjoys many different kinds of flowers and will visit as many as 90 different flowers in 1 day. Some of this butterfly's favorite flowers are bougainvillea, hibiscus, bouncing bet, swamp milkweed, and lantana.

Average Adult Life Span: 9 to 14 days

Our example: 10 days in a giant swallowtail lifetime × 90 flowers visited each day = 900 flowers visited in a lifetime.

Spotted Seahorse *Hippocampus kuda*

Spotted seahorses are fish that live in shallow coastal seawater in the southeast Pacific. They have prehensile tails that hold on to seaweed or coral. Their fins and coloring help them blend into their habitat and remain unnoticed. This allows these seahorses to get close to their prey of brine shrimp or baby crabs. The spotted seahorses eat by sucking their prey through their tube-shaped mouths.

Every few months, a female deposits 100 to 250 eggs into a brood pouch on the male seahorse's front. The male fertilizes the eggs and carries them for 3 to 4 weeks until they hatch. Then he births baby seahorses, called fry, into the sea. The male seahorse is the only male animal that births live young.

Average Adult Life Span: 1 to 2 years in the wild

Our example: Female makes 4 deposits of eggs totaling, on average, 675 eggs for 1 year. Average life span of 1½ years for a male spotted seahorse × 675 fry = 1,012½ seahorse babies in a lifetime. Rounding 1,012½ fry to the nearest hundred = 1,000 seahorse babies.

WHAT IS AN AVERAGE?

The word *average* refers to a typical or usual amount. You might brush your teeth, on the average, 3 times a day. Some days when you're away from home, you might brush only twice. Other days when you eat a few extra snacks, you might brush your teeth 4 times. 3 is the typical number of times that you brush your teeth each day.

As I wrote this book, I needed a handy way to show the typical or usual number of times that an animal does 1 behavior—like how many baby kangaroos a mother kangaroo will birth each year. Sometimes she births 2 babies a year, and sometimes it's 3 babies per year.

Here's how to find an average. Add the numbers you have together, and then divide that amount by how many numbers you added together. With baby kangaroos, we have the numbers 2 and 3. If we add them together (2 + 3 = 5), then we need to divide 5 by 2 (5 ÷ 2 = 2½). On average, the mother kangaroo has 2½ babies per year. (That doesn't mean she birthed half a baby in that year, it means she was halfway through the process of making a baby.)

Returning to our example of brushing teeth, let's pretend that this was your schedule for 7 days, or 1 week:

Sunday	4 times
Monday	2 times
Tuesday	3 times
Wednesday	2 times
Thursday	3 times
Friday	3 times
Saturday	4 times

If we add all the numbers together, we would get 21. Then, we would divide 21 by the number of days listed, which is 7 (21 ÷ 7 = 3). For that particular week, you brushed your teeth 3 times a day on average.

I LOVE MATH

Math gives you answers you can't find any other way. Without math, I wouldn't have been able to write this book. It's true!

I was curious about animals' lives. I wanted to know things that I couldn't find in a book or on the Internet. But all the clues I needed were there.

In fact, the process of finding the facts I needed was more like solving a problem—a story problem. Let me show you.

One of the animals that I researched was the American lobster (**Homarus americanus**). I wanted to know how many times this animal sheds its exoskeleton in 1 lifetime. To figure this out, I first needed to know the average life span of an American lobster. Most experts agreed that 65 to 70 years is the average—although some lobsters do live to be 100 years old! I used 70 years as my average lifetime.

I learned that this species of lobsters molts at different rates depending on its age. For instance, in the first year of its life, it grows very fast and sheds its exoskeleton 40 times. But as it matures, it grows more slowly and molts less and less. Between its first and eighth years, it will shed its exoskeleton 24 times. Between its ninth and twenty-fourth years, it will molt 8 times. By the time this lobster is 25 years old, it sheds its exoskeleton only once every 5 years on the average. And, from its twenty-fifth through seventieth years, it will molt only 8 more times.

I added all of those numbers: 40 + 24 + 8 + 8 = 80. That means an average American lobster will shed its exoskeleton 80 times in 1 lifetime. Amazing!

Now, it's your turn. See if you can solve these problems. Good luck!

Answer key below.

2 An average southern three-banded armadillo (*Tolypeutes matacus*) lives 14 years. Zoologists estimate that this armadillo will roll into a ball to protect itself 52 times a year. However, in the first 6 months of its life, it doesn't roll at all. Approximately how many times does an armadillo roll into a ball in its lifetime? Round your answer to the nearest hundred, please.

3 A female Florida bark scorpion's (*Centruroides gracilis*) life span is approximately 3½ years (42 months). She will birth 2 broods of scorplings (baby scorpions) a year. Each brood contains an average of 47 scorplings. As soon as they are born, the scorplings crawl on their mother's back for protection until they molt. How many scorplings will a female Florida bark scorpion carry on her back in one lifetime? Round your answer to the nearest ten, please.

18 84 93
34
55
670 26 50
9
12 77 332
61
43 5 24

861

546

2

94

639

900

4

62

3

27

7

46

1000

249

81

50

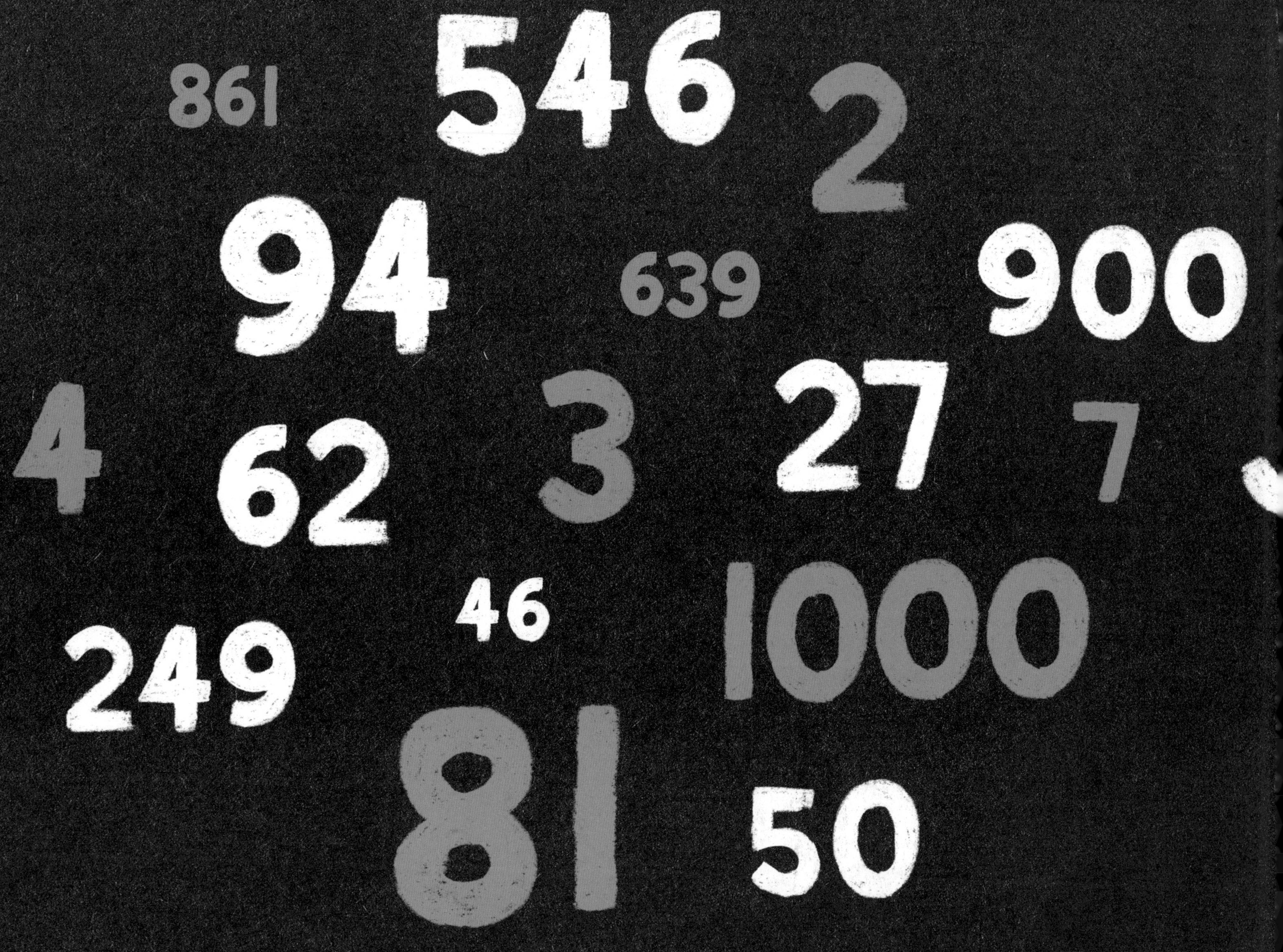